John the Baptist

Saint for Baptism

First century
Born in the hill country of Judea
Feast Days: June 24 (Birth)
August 29 (Martyrdom)
Patron saint of the Sacrament of Baptism,
converts, and the country Jordan

Text by Barbara Yoffie
Illustrated by Jeff Albrecht

Liguori
PUBLICATIONS
A Redemptorist Ministry

Dedication

To my family:
my parents Jim and Peg,
my husband Bill,
our son Sam and daughter-in-law Erin,
and our precious grandchildren
Ben, Lucas, and Andrew

To all the children I have had the privilege
of teaching throughout the years.

Imprimi Potest:
Stephen T. Rehrauer, CSsR, Provincial
Denver Province, the Redemptorists

Imprimatur:
In accordance with CIC 827, permission to publish has been granted on September 28, 2018, by the Most Reverend Mark S. Rivituso, Auxiliary Bishop, Archdiocese of St. Louis. Permission to publish is an indication that nothing contrary to Church teaching is contained in this work. It does not imply any endorsement of the opinions expressed in the publication; nor is any liability assumed by this permission.

Published by Liguori Publications, Liguori, Missouri 63057
To order, visit Liguori.org or call 800-325-9521.
Copyright © 2018 Liguori Publications

ISBN 978-0-7648-2796-9

Liguori Publications, a nonprofit corporation, is an apostolate of the Redemptorists. To learn more about the Redemptorists, visit Redemptorists.com.

Printed in the United States of America
22 21 20 19 18 / 5 4 3 2 1
First Edition

Dear Parents and Teachers:

Saints and Me! is a series of children's books about saints, with six books apiece in the first four sets. The first set, *Saints of North America,* honors holy men and women who blessed and served the land we call home. The second, *Saints of Christmas,* includes heavenly heroes who inspire us through Advent and Christmas and teach us to love the Infant Jesus. The third, *Saints for Families,* introduces saints who modeled God's love within and for the domestic Church. The fourth, *Saints for Communities,* explores individuals from different times and places who served Jesus through their various roles and professions.

The seven books in the *Saints for Sacraments* series explore eight saints who had great love for the sacraments. John the Baptist baptized Jesus in the Jordan River. Padre Pio helped people make a good confession. Teresa of Ávila was known for her great love of the Eucharist. Philip Neri received the Holy Spirit after praying to God. Louis and Zélie Martin, a married couple, taught their children to serve God and the poor. At an early age, John Vianney wanted to dedicate his life to God as a priest; today he is the patron saint of parish priests. Maximilian Kolbe battled poor health to become a priest and brought God's healing to sick people.

Name the saint who lived in the desert and ate locusts and honey. In this set of books, who was the saint with stigmata? Who began a Carmelite convent dedicated to prayer? Who grew up during the French Revolution? Which saints were the parents of Thérèse of Lisieux? Who volunteered to die in place of a stranger in a prison camp? Find out in the *Saints for Sacraments* set—part of the *Saints and Me!* series—and help children connect to the lives of the saints.

Introduce your children or students to the *Saints and Me!* series as they:

—READ about the lives of the saints and are inspired by their stories.

—PRAY to the saints for their intercession.

—CELEBRATE the saints and relate them to their lives.

saints for
sacraments

John the Baptist
Baptism

Teresa of Ávila
Eucharist

Philip Neri
Confirmation

padre pio
Reconciliation

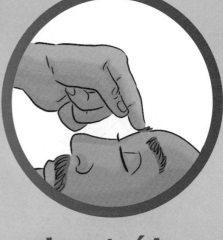

maximilian kolbe
Anointing of the Sick

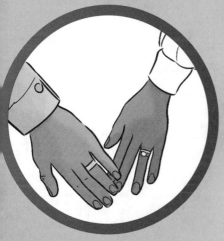

louis and zélie martin
Matrimony

john vianney
Holy Orders

John was a great prophet and preacher who lived a long time ago. Because he baptized a lot of people, he was called John the Baptist. He baptized Jesus! Baptism is the first sacrament we receive. When we are baptized, original sin is washed away and the Holy Spirit comes to us for the first time. We become children of God and members of the Church.

Zechariah and Elizabeth were John's parents. They were good and holy people. Together they prayed that they would someday have a baby to love. They waited for a very long time. Then one day, something amazing happened!

Zechariah was praying in the Temple. The angel Gabriel appeared to him and said, "Your wife, Elizabeth, is going to have a baby boy. You will name him John." Zechariah and Elizabeth were really happy! Their baby was very special. God had chosen John for a special mission. John would tell everybody about Jesus, the Messiah!

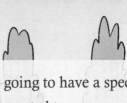

Elizabeth's cousin, Mary, was also going to have a special baby, Jesus, the Son of God. Mary wanted to go see Elizabeth. She hurried to her house far away. Elizabeth was so excited to see Mary. Her baby recognized Jesus and moved inside her. He was happy, too!

"Oh Mary, you are blessed by God," said Elizabeth. "My heart is full of joy," replied Mary. Mary stayed to help Elizabeth for about three months and then went home.

When John grew up, he went to live in the desert. His life was very simple. He ate whatever he could find, usually locusts and wild honey. John wore clothes made from camel's hair and tied a belt around his waist. He prayed and listened for God's voice. After a long time, John was ready to do God's work.

John traveled to the Jordan River. Here he preached to the people. "Jesus the Messiah is coming soon! Get ready!" John told the crowds. "Share what you have with others. Be kind and fair," he said. Many people listened to him and followed him. His followers were called disciples.

John told people to repent and make up for their sins. Some people did not like what John said. They turned and walked away shaking their heads. Others wanted to get ready for Jesus. They were sorry for their sins and changed their hearts and lives. John baptized them. Today the waters of baptism give new life in Jesus. You become Jesus' friend.

Soon John was called John the Baptist. People asked him, "Who are you? Are you the Messiah?" "No, someone else is coming, and you must get ready," John the Baptist answered. Then he said, "I am not worthy to carry his sandals. I baptize you with water, he will baptize with the Holy Spirit."

Then one day, Jesus came to the Jordan River. He listened to John the Baptist preach to the crowds by the river. He saw people being baptized. Jesus, though sinless, told John the Baptist he wanted to be baptized! John the Baptist said, "Jesus, you should baptize me!" Jesus said, "I need to be baptized by you." He wanted to be baptized so that we would become God's adopted sons and daughters.

John the Baptist smiled. He reached out to Jesus and baptized him in the Jordan River. At that moment, heaven opened. The Holy Spirit came down as a dove. And a voice came from heaven, "You are my Son. I am pleased with you."

Now it was time for Jesus to travel to different towns to preach and teach. Many people followed him. *"I must let Jesus do his work,"* thought John the Baptist. He told his disciples, "My work is finished now. Jesus is the Messiah. You must follow him, not me."

John the Baptist stayed in the Jordan valley and preached for some time. He reminded people to live holy lives. He even reminded the bad king, Herod Antipas, how he should live! The king shouted, "I am the king and I can do what I want! I will not do what John the Baptist tells me."

King Herod Antipas put John the Baptist in jail. John the Baptist was not afraid to speak the truth about the faith. Jesus was the center of his life and his preaching. He wanted everyone to get ready for Jesus, so he shared his message with all the people. "Repent! Be baptized! Turn away from sin and turn to Jesus. He will show you how to be holy."

Later, the king had John the Baptist put to death. The Church honors John the Baptist as a martyr, a hero of the faith.

The sacrament of baptism washes away the sin we have from birth, strengthens us, and gives us God's grace, God's life, and God's love. This grace helps us live holy lives so we can do God's work. We can help people know and love Jesus, just like Saint John the Baptist!

Teach about Jesus and share what you know.
Tell others his message so their faith will grow.

Saint John the Baptist.
You told people to repent.
You changed people's
hearts and lives
so they could follow Jesus.
Open my heart
to do god's work
so I may grow
in holiness and love.
Amen.

GLOSSARY (New Words)

Angel: A spiritual being; God's helper and messenger

Baptism: The sacrament that makes us children of God and members of the Church

Disciple: A person who follows the teachings of a great leader

Herod Antipas: The son of Herod the Great, who was king when Jesus was born

Holy Spirit: The third person of the Blessed Trinity

Locust: A large grasshopper

Martyr: Someone who gives up his or her life for a belief or a cause

Messiah: Jesus, the Son of God and Savior of the world

Original sin: The first sin committed by the first man and woman; the first sin that affects every person throughout history

Preach: To teach about the faith

Prophet: Someone God calls to give a special message

Repent: To turn away from sin and ask for God's help to live a holy life

Sacrament: Seven special signs of God's life and love

Temple: A place of worship and learning for the Jews